ORIENTAL CARPET DESIGNS
In Full Color

BY
FRIEDRICH SARRE
AND
HERMANN TRENKWALD

Dover Publications, Inc.
New York

Published in Canada by General Publishing Company, Ltd., 30 Lesmill Road, Don Mills, Toronto, Ontario.
Published in the United Kingdom by Constable and Company, Ltd., 10 Orange Street, London WC2H 7EG.

Oriental Carpet Designs in Full Color, first published by Dover Publications, Inc., in 1979, is a new selection of plates (with various reduction and cropping) from: *Old Oriental Carpets / Issued by / The Austrian Museum for Art and Industry / with Text by / Friedrich Sarre and Hermann Trenkwald / Translated by A. F. Kendrick,* originally published in two volumes, 1926 and 1929, by Anton Schroll & Co., Vienna, and Karl W. Hiersemann, Leipzig. The captions and Notes on the Plates, based on the original text, were prepared specially for the present edition.

DOVER *Pictorial Archive* SERIES

International Standard Book Number: 0-486-23835-0
Library of Congress Catalog Card Number: 79-52102

Manufactured in the United States of America
Dover Publications, Inc.
180 Varick Street
New York, N.Y. 10014

PREFACE AND NOTES ON THE PLATES

The plates in this book, based on actual color photographs of the original carpets, have been selected from one of the most outstanding publications on the subject. Written by two eminent German scholars and translated with additional comments by an English specialist, *Old Oriental Carpets* (1926 and 1929) assembled within two volumes some of the most highly prized pieces in European and American public and private collections: not merely fine representative examples but pinnacles of carpet-making achievement from Persia and such other major areas as India, Turkey and the Caucasus. The information that follows concerning the individual carpets in the present volume is a brief condensation of the original descriptive text; the ownership given in parentheses at the end of each note is unaltered from the 1926–1929 publication.

Inside front cover: Asia Minor or the Caucasus. First half of the 15th century. 172 x 90 cm. The border is missing at the right, and its outer bands at the left. The stylized animal figures probably represent the ancient Chinese motif of the struggle between dragon and phoenix. (Department of Islamic Art of the National Museums, Berlin.)

Page 1: Persia. Second half of the 16th century. 124 x 109 cm. The field has a scattered pattern of flowering shrubs with single or grouped animals in three transverse rows. The main border consists of two intersecting wavy stems with blossoms, buds, palmettes and lion's masks. This type of carpet is stylistically connected with the gold marginal paintings on colored paper in Persian manuscripts of the period. (Louvre, Paris.)

Page 2: "Portuguese" carpet from Persia. 17th century. Whole carpet 677 x 372 cm, part shown includes full width. The color zones emanating from the large central panel, all filled with birds and flowers, cover almost the entire field. Each corner shows two sailing vessels, manned at least partially by Iberians. A man is seen swimming in the water. The border has an arabesque stem. The carpet may have been woven for Portugal or Goa, and may record an actual event. (Austrian Museum for Art and Industry, Vienna.)

Page 3: Central Persia. First half of the 17th century. Whole carpet 397 x 136 cm, part shown includes full width. Brocaded in gold and silver. The field has an allover pattern of four-sided compartments, every four of them enclosing another. The main border contains a wavy stem. (John D. Rockefeller, Jr., New York.)

Pages 4 & 5: North Persia. Mid-16th century. Whole carpet 818 x 372 cm, part shown 580 x 372 cm. The central lozenge contains 44 cranes and four antelopes. Each corner panel has two winged genii in Chinese costume. Numerous animals appear among the trees on the light ground. The main border has an intermittent wavy stem. (Clarence H. Mackay, Long Island, New York.)

Page 6: Persia. 17th or 18th century. Whole carpet 910 x 245 cm, part shown includes full width. The field has an allover pattern of lozenge forms in five longitudinal rows, the pattern being repeated after every four latitudinal rows. In the main border, cup palmettes alternate with fan palmettes on a wavy stem. (Austrian Museum for Art and Industry, Vienna.)

Page 7: Vase carpet from Persia. 17th century. Whole carpet 610 x 255 cm, part shown includes full width. The field has an allover repeat in parallel rows, vase motifs alternating with candelabra motifs. The border has a wavy stem with palmettes. (Austrian Museum for Art and Industry, Vienna.)

Page 8: N.W. Persia. Woven 1542/3 in a workshop directed by Ghiyath ud-Din Jami (according to inscription in central cartouche). Whole carpet 570 x 365 cm, part shown 440 x 330 cm. The field contains a central panel and quarter-panels at the four corners, all ornamented with flowers, plants and birds. The main ground has hunting scenes, each quarter containing seven riders and one huntsman on foot, in pursuit of antelopes, bears, wild asses, lions, lynxes, boars, stags and other animals. (Poldi-Pezzoli Museum, Milan.)

Page 9: Hunting carpet of the Persian court manufactory. Second half of the 16th century. Whole carpet 695 x 323 cm. This detail shows a corner ornament of the field (a quadrant of the star in the center of the field, it contains dragons and phoenixes), part of the main ground design (huntsmen on 58 horses pursue 173 wild animals) and part of the border (in the main band are pairs of Persian genii). This is the most celebrated old Persian carpet. (Austrian Museum for Art and Industry, Vienna.)

Page 10: A closer detail of the carpet on page 9—genii from the main border band.

Page 11: A closer detail of the carpet on page 9—a bowman from the main ground of the field.

Page 12: "Ushak" carpet from Asia Minor. About 1600. 400 x 203 cm. Three red serrated panels enclosing stylized flowers; star forms cut off by the border; and a ground of angular floral stems constitute the field. Arabesque stems fill the middle band of the border. (Austrian Museum for Art and Industry, Vienna.)

Page 13: India. About 1600. 235 x 156 cm. Many kinds of birds appear in a freely composed wooded landscape. The main border features palmettes enclosing animal heads, separated by cartouches flanked by leopards. (Austrian Museum for Art and Industry, Vienna.)

Page 14: India. About 1600. Whole carpet 923 x 338 cm, part shown 456 x 338 cm. The field has a repeating pattern of longitudinal rows of palmettes, oriented in different directions. The main border has a pattern of panels of various shapes. (Pierpont Morgan Collection, Metropolitan Museum of Art, New York.)

Page 15: India. First half of the 17th century. Whole carpet 406 x 167 cm, part shown 220 x 167 cm. The central longitudinal row of the field alternates dark cartouches with yellowish eight-pointed stars. The similar rows to the right and left are bisected by the border. The panels are separated by large palmettes, themselves separated by large blossoms. The border features naturalistically drawn plants. (Altman Collection, Metropolitan Museum of Art, New York.)

Page 16: Vase carpet from Persia. 16th century. Whole carpet 248 x 150 cm, part shown includes full width. The field has an allover pattern of floral motifs in four distinct systems. The border has intersecting wavy arabesque stems. (Austrian Museum for Art and Industry, Vienna.)

Page 17: "Garden" carpet from N.W. or central Persia. First half of the 16th century. 187 x 151 cm. The bands that separate the six compartments of the field represent water channels, as shown by the small blue waves, the fish and the ducks. Each compartment contains a central cartouche and two bisected cartouches, as well as flowers, or birds in trees. (Albert Figdor, Vienna.)

Page 18: North Persia (?). End of the 16th century. Whole carpet 783 x 379 cm, part shown 453 x 252 cm. In the green inner star of the central panel are gazelles and leopards. The red zone outside of that has phoenix and dragon combats. Numerous trees, animals and hunters symmetrically fill the ground. The field has no corner elements. The middle band of the border features more phoenixes and dragons. (Louvre, Paris.)

Page 19: Landscape carpet from India. First half of the 17th century. 243 x 151 cm. At the top of the field are buildings enlivened with figures (a temple at the upper right). Next come fighting animals. Then come hunters returning home. Next is a fabulous beast that has seized seven elephants but is attacked by a phoenix. At the bottom a lion-dragon chases two steinbocks. The disconnected scenes were obviously copied from several miniature paintings. The border features demon masks. (Museum of Fine Arts, Boston.)

Page 20 & 21: Persia. Second half of the 16th century. Whole carpet 225 x 158 cm. Shown is part of the border—containing a love poem to a beautiful woman—and the entire inner field, in which the central panel has arabesque stems, the corner panels have birds on branches, and the ground has various animals amid plant life. (Von Pannwitz, Hartekamp, Holland.)

Page 22: North Persia. About 1500. Whole carpet 498 x 340 cm, part shown includes full width. The field has a mosaic pattern of panels in regularly repeating groups. The large central panel of each group of nine depicts the combat between the dragon and the phoenix. The main border features long cartouches and eight-lobed circles. (Metropolitan Museum of Art, New York.)

Page 23: North Persia. 1539/40 (dated in the cartouche seen at the lower left of the plate). From the tomb-mosque of Sheikh Safi at Ardabil. Whole carpet 1152 x 534 cm, part shown 530 x 310 cm. This is one of the most renowned carpets of the greatest period. Seen in the plate is one of the two mosque lamps that hang from the central panel, one of the corners with a quarter-section of the central panel, and a portion of the field with its spiraling flowery stems. Made for a mosque, the carpet lacks human and animal figures. (Victoria & Albert Museum, London.)

Page 24: Turkish court manufactory. 16th century. Whole carpet 436 x 248 cm. This detail shows a corner of the field, with one of the corner half-arabesque panels and part of the leafwork radiating from one of the three central cartouches; as well as a portion of the border (the broadest band has two alternating types of palmette). (Austrian Museum for Art and Industry, Vienna.)

Page 25: "Herati" carpet from eastern Persia. 16th or 17th century. Whole carpet 530 x 255 cm. Close spiral stems cover the field, with some lozenge motifs and a suggestion of parallel bands. The middle band of the border has an intermittent wavy blossoming stem interrupted by palmettes. (Austrian Museum for Art and Industry, Vienna.)

Page 26: Animal carpet from Persia. 16th century. Whole carpet 183 x 126 cm. The field is basically a double system of curling stems with flowers, buds, leaves and palmettes. Among them are various real and mythical animals. The middle band of the border has an intermittent wavy stem, ogee-shaped compartments containing palmettes, and red arabesque bands. (Austrian Museum for Art and Industry, Vienna.)

Page 27: Animal carpet from Persia. Mid-16th century. 238 x 179 cm. Six transverse rows of animals, including such fabulous beasts as the lion-dragon and stag-dragon, are seen against a field of flowering shrubs and trees. The main border contains wavy stems, with palmettes at their intersections and pheasant-like birds flanking alternate palmettes. (Altman Collection, Metropolitan Museum of Art, New York.)

Page 28: "Armenian" carpet from the Caucasus. First half of the 17th century. Whole carpet 465 x 195 cm, part shown includes full width. An allover stem pattern covers the field, featuring palmettes, rosettes and stylized irises. The border has broken S-form wavy stems, palmettes and rosettes. (Austrian Museum for Art and Industry, Vienna.)

Page 29: The Graf carpet, a "dragon" carpet from eastern Asia Minor or the Caucasus. 15th century. Whole carpet 678 x 230 cm, part shown 320 x 230 cm. The field consists of five longitudinal rows of lozenges containing animals, single or in pairs, sometimes separated by a tree or stem. (Department of Islamic Art of the National Museums, Berlin.)

Page 30: Persia. Mid-17th century. 190 x 134.5 cm. The field contains rows of flowering shrubs, with flowering trees at the corners. The central band of the three-part border features a wavy stem intercepted by palmettes. (Dr. J. Goldschmidt, Berlin.)

Page 31: Central Persia. First half of the 17th century. 216 x 136 cm. Brocaded in gold and silver. The field is compartmented with panels of different shapes and directions. The main border has an elongated floral stem, palmettes, blossoms and leaves. (John D. Rockefeller, Jr., New York.)

Page 32: Prayer carpet of the Turkish court manufactory. 16th century. 185 x 117 cm. The inner field is in the form of a prayer niche with a horseshoe arch at the top. Palmettes replace the usual architectonic supports. The niche is filled with a bold floral composition. (Austrian Museum for Art and Industry, Vienna.)

Page 33: Prayer carpet from India. 17th century. 155 x 107 cm. The field represents a prayer niche with a pointed scalloped arch. A large composite flowering plant, springing from a low mound, covers the main ground. The middle band of the border has elaborately interlocking floral stems. (Austrian Museum for Art and Industry, Vienna.)

Page 34: Central Persia. First half of the 17th century. 257 x 130 cm. Tapestry-woven. Each corner of the field contains a quarter-section of the oval central panel, which features flying cranes. The blue cartouches and red finials that flank the central panel contain pairs of ducks. The ground is covered with blossoming plants (it is unusual that they are placed transversely) and groups of animals. Birds and animals fill the border cartouches. The illustration here omits the long bottom fringe. (Private collection, Chicago.)

Page 35: Persia. First half of the 17th century. Whole carpet 389 x 152 cm, part shown 50 x 152 cm. This portion of the field shows the central panel with a crowned genius served by 12 attendant genii; one of the two flanking cartouches with calligraphy; several of the hunting scenes in the main ground; and portions of other panels. (Residenzmuseum, Munich.)

Pages 36 & 37, above: Same carpet as on page 35. This is one of the two borders on the short sides. In the middle band two steinbocks fight in an octofoil that is flanked by two cartouches with genii. The outer bands (like the field cartouches) contain love verses with constant allusions to carpets.

Pages 36 & 37, below: India. About 1600. Whole carpet 347 x 133 cm, part shown includes full width. This Indo-Persian carpet is of "Herati" pattern, with a double stem design forming an allover repeat. The longitudinal middle line, flanked by palmettes, is accentuated. The border has two rows of half-panels with floral fillings. (Austrian Museum for Art and Industry, Vienna.)

Page 38: Arabesque carpet from Persia. 16th century. Fragment, 210 x 289 cm. The field has an allover pattern of two series of arabesque stems intersecting in a network. Flowering plants grow between and beneath the stems. The main border has further wavy blossoming arabesque stems with white flowers in the open spaces. (Austrian Museum for Art and Industry, Vienna.)

Page 39: Asia Minor. End of the 18th century. Fragmentary; 305 x 150 cm. Two broad wavy stems run from end to end. The branches have serrated leaves and stylized flowers. There was never a border. (Austrian Museum for Art and Industry, Vienna.)

Page 40: Persia. 16th–17th century. Whole carpet 735 x 300 cm, part shown includes full width. The field has an allover pattern, with three longitudinal rows of larger and smaller oval rosettes and palmettes flanked by rows of fan and fringed palmettes. The main border band has palmettes and interlocking arabesques. (Austrian Museum for Art and Industry, Vienna.)

Page 41: North Persia. About 1550. Whole carpet 540 x 270 cm, part shown 166 cm wide. The field contains an allover pattern of alternating rows of quatrefoil and trefoil panels (three rows and two halves in the width, seven rows and two halves in the length). Every other trefoil panel contains confronted pheasants or peacocks. Flowering and fruiting trees fill the spaces between panels. (Franz Graf Clam Gallas, Vienna.)

Page 42: North Persia. First half of the 16th century. Whole carpet 570 x 270 cm, part shown 400 x 270 cm. The lozenge-shaped central panel contains a circular space representing a pool (clouds, waves and ducks). The smaller white oblong panels flanking the central panel contain confronted peacocks. The main field shows blossoming trees and cypresses, with birds and animals among them. (Prince Schwarzenberg, Vienna.)

Page 43: North Persia. Mid-16th century. Whole carpet 427 x 186 cm, part shown includes full width. The central panel contains a quatrain about the carpet in the loved one's room. Peacocks appear in the smaller panel just above it. The corner panels have animals and fish. The main ground is full of animals. The oblong border cartouches contain an ode that can be applied equally well to a beautiful adolescent boy or to the carpet itself. (George F. Baker, New York; on loan to Metropolitan Museum of Art, New York.)

Page 44: "Armenian" carpet from the Caucasus. End of the 17th century. 298 x 167 cm. The field consists of a large stem and cartouches, making three longitudinal rows of floral motifs. The middle border band has serrated leaves and cup-shaped blossoms on a wavy stem. (Austrian Museum for Art and Industry, Vienna.)

Inside back cover: Asia Minor. About 1600. 255 x 156 cm. The field is covered with an allover pattern of angular foliage in three longitudinal rows. The border has a row of panels containing stylized plant forms. (Austrian Museum for Art and Industry, Vienna.)

Persia. Second half of the 16th century.

"Portuguese" carpet from Persia. 17th century.

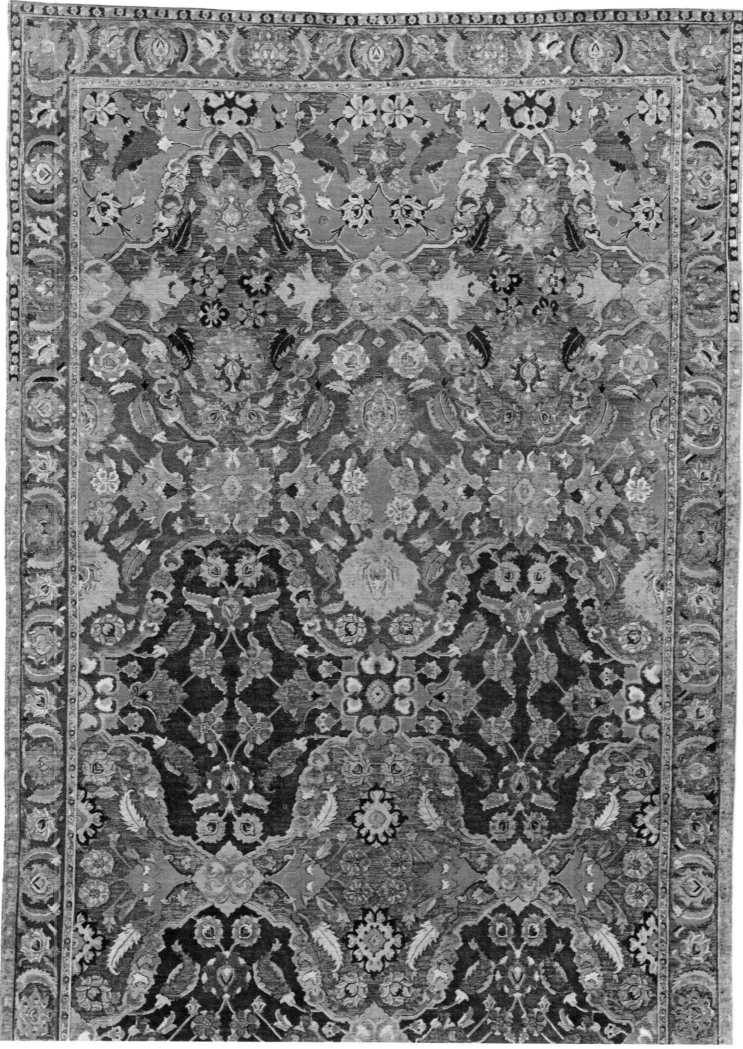

Central Persia. First half of the 17th century.

4

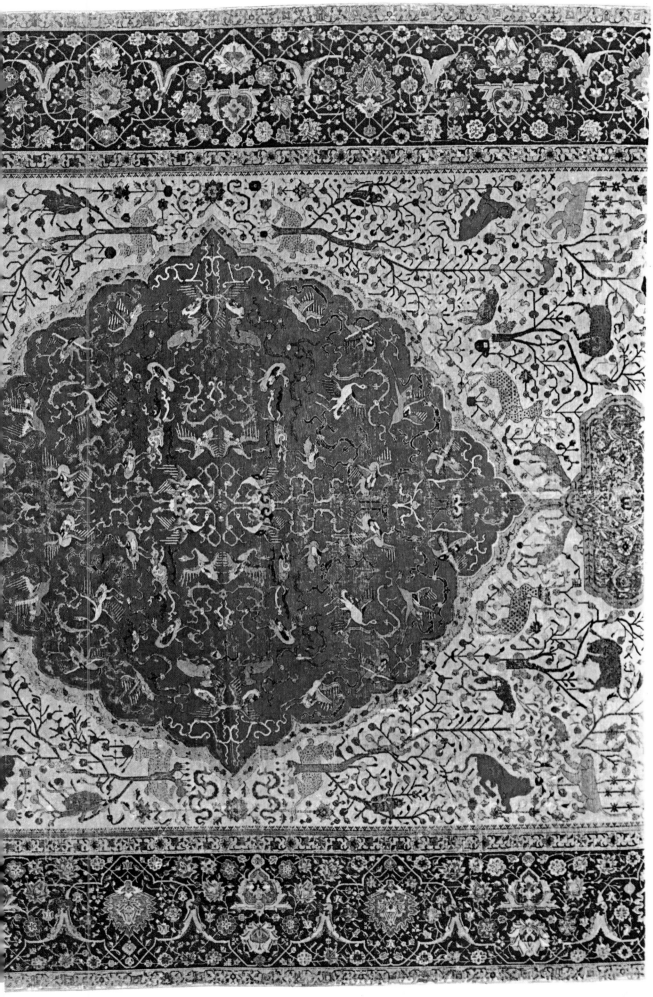

North Persia. Mid-16th century.

Persia. 17th or 18th century.

Vase carpet from Persia. 17th century.

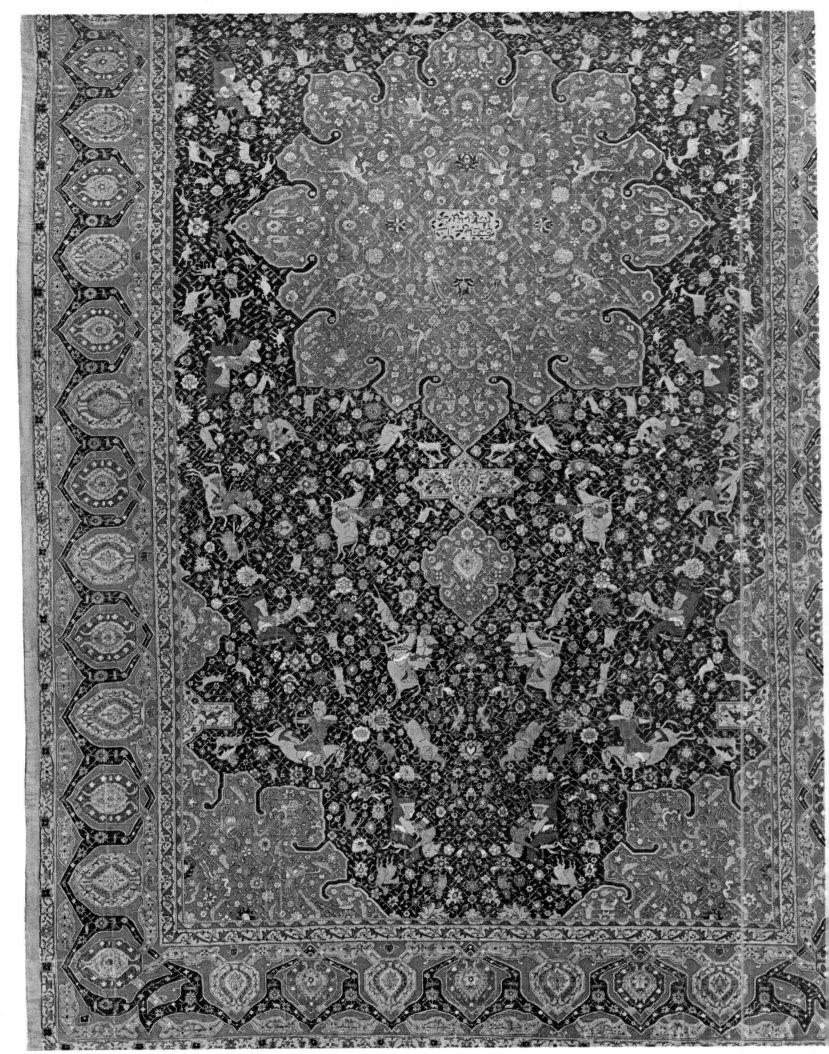

N.W. Persia. 1542/3.

Hunting carpet of the Persian court manufactory. Second half of the 16th century.

Detail of the preceding carpet: genii from the main border band.

Another detail of the same carpet: a bowman from the main ground of the field.

"Ushak" carpet from Asia Minor. About 1600.

India. About 1600.

India. About 1600.

India. First half of the 17th century.

Vase carpet from Persia. 16th century.

"Garden" carpet from N.W. or central Persia. First half of the 16th century.

North Persia (?). End of the 16th century.

Landscape carpet from India. First half of the 17th century.

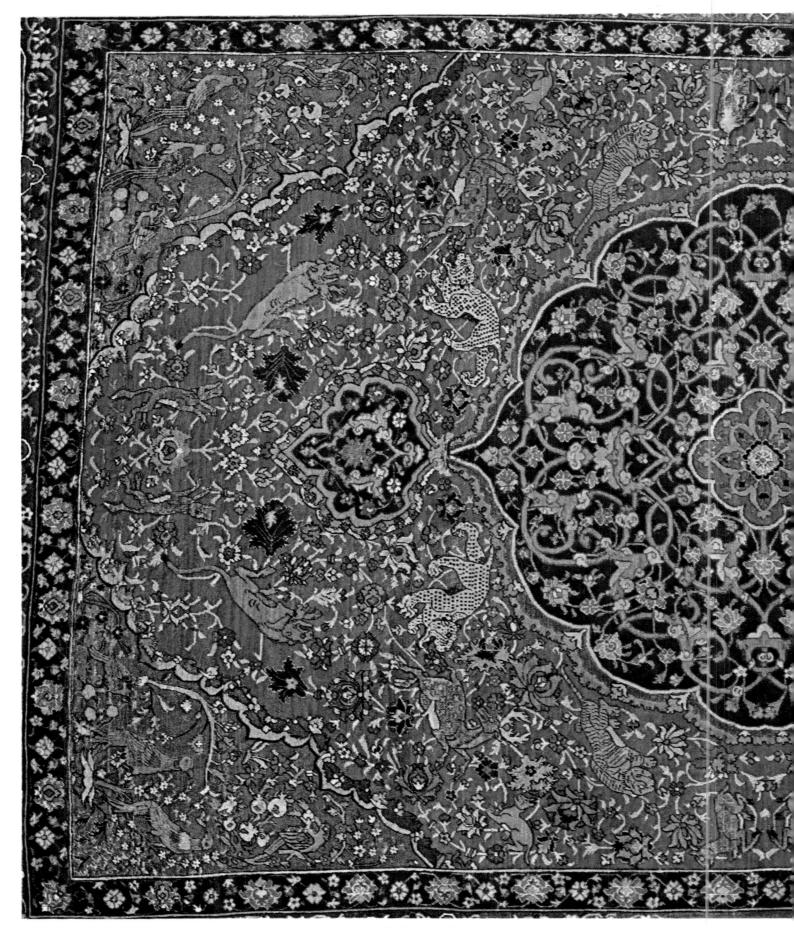

Persia. Second half of the 16th century.

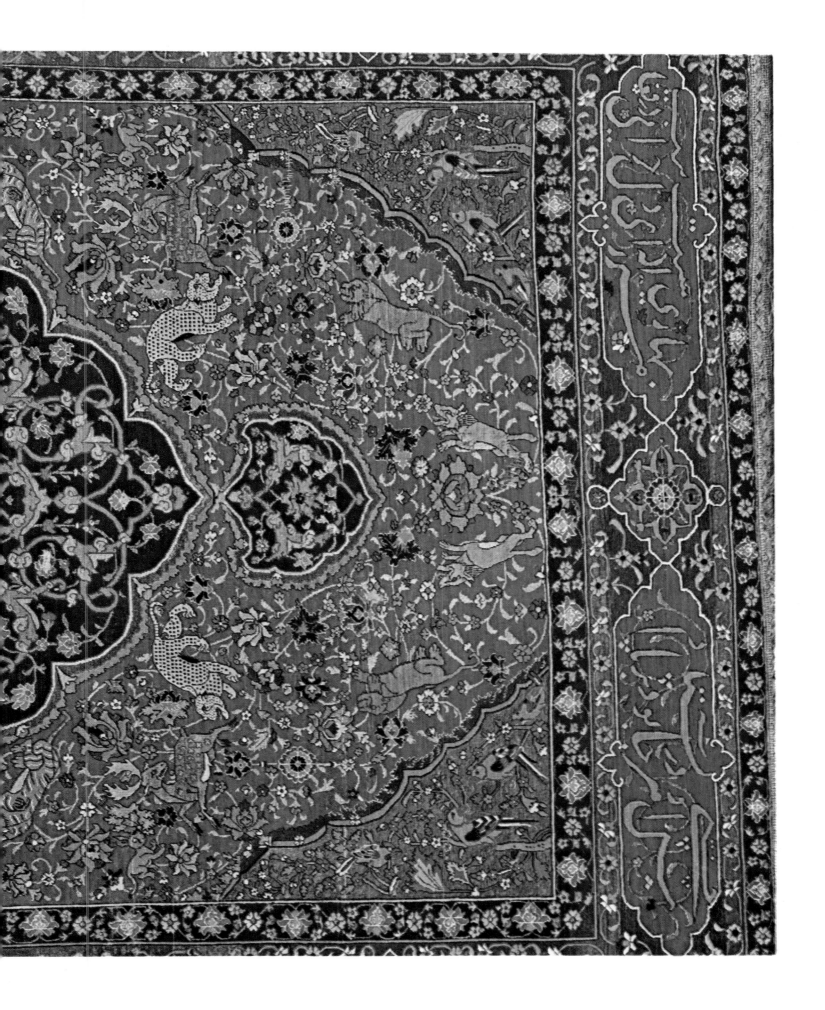

North Persia. About 1500.

North Persia. 1539/40.

Turkish court manufactory. 16th century.

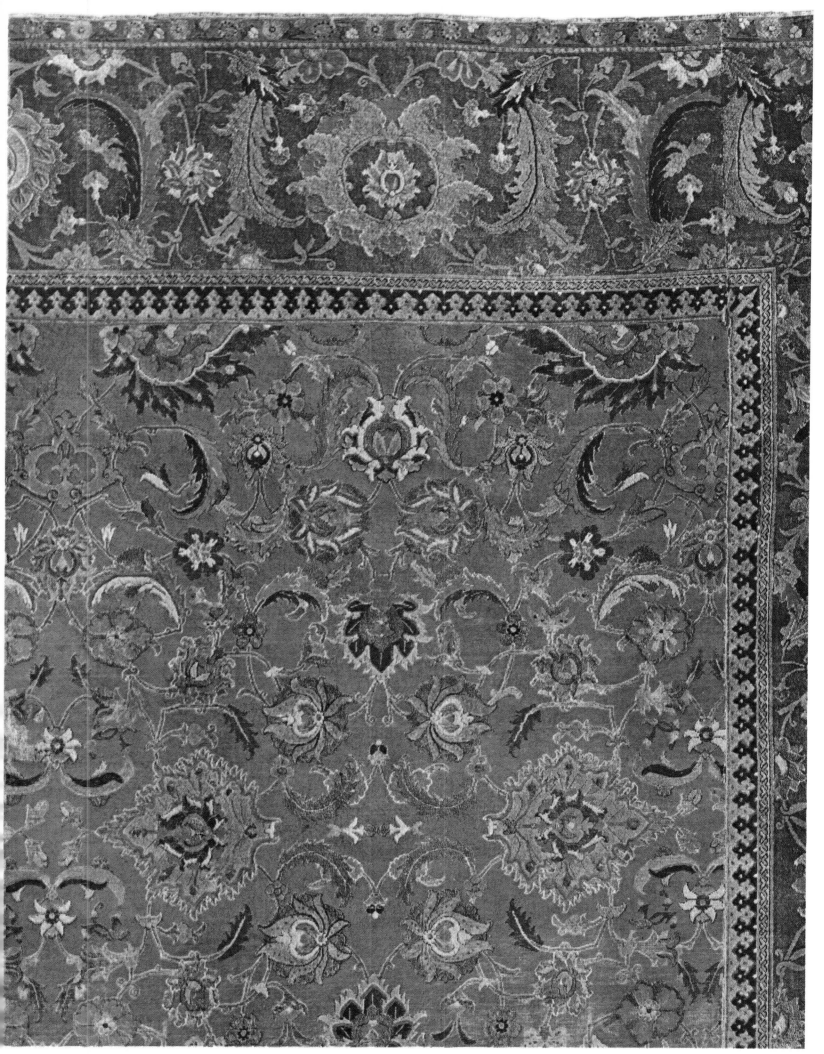

"Herati" carpet from eastern Persia. 16th or 17th century.

Animal carpet from Persia. 16th century.

Animal carpet from Persia. Mid-16th century.

"Armenian" carpet from the Caucasus. First half of the 17th century.

The Graf carpet, a "dragon" carpet from eastern Asia Minor or the Caucasus.
15th century.

Persia. Mid-17th century.

Central Persia. First half of the 17th century.

Prayer carpet of the Turkish court manufactory. 16th century.

Prayer carpet from India. 17th century.

Central Persia. First half of the 17th century.

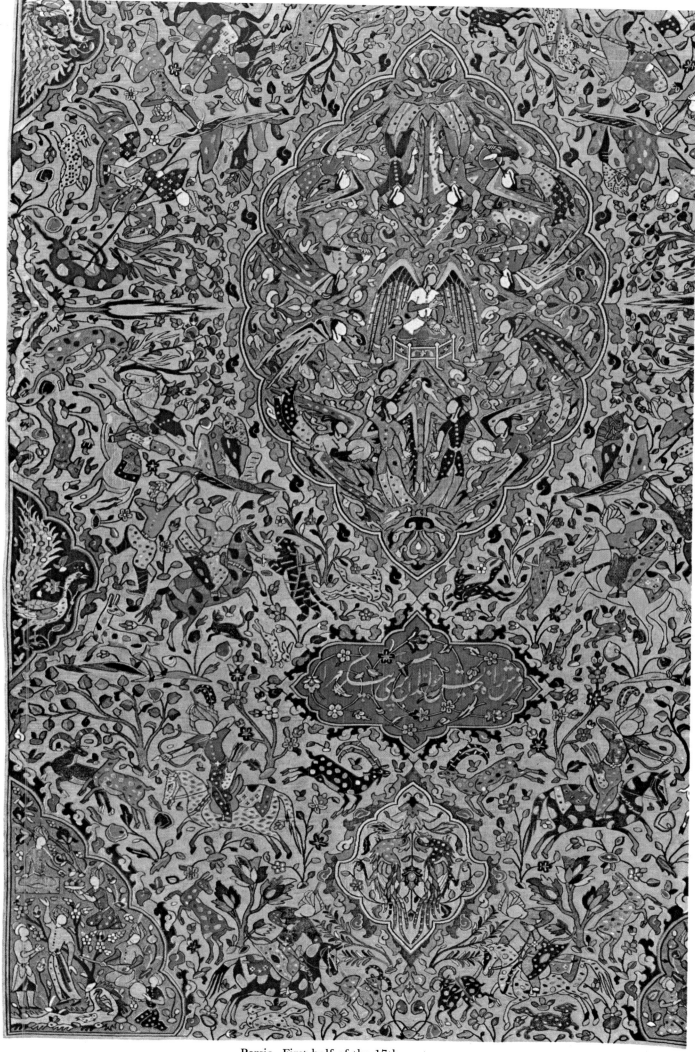

Persia. First half of the 17th century.

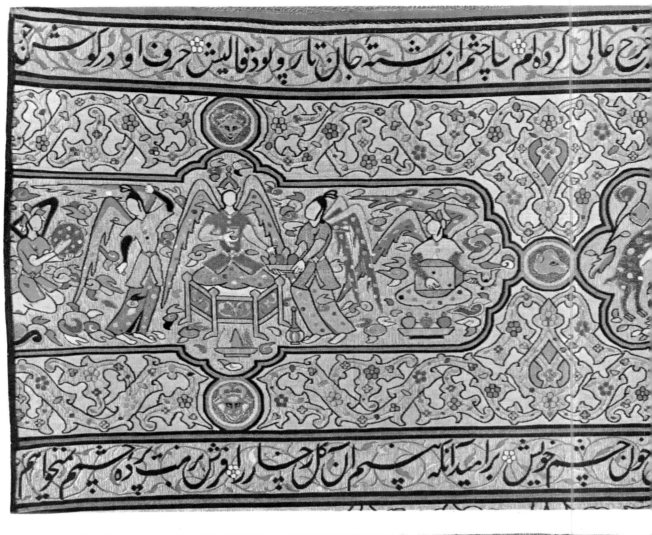

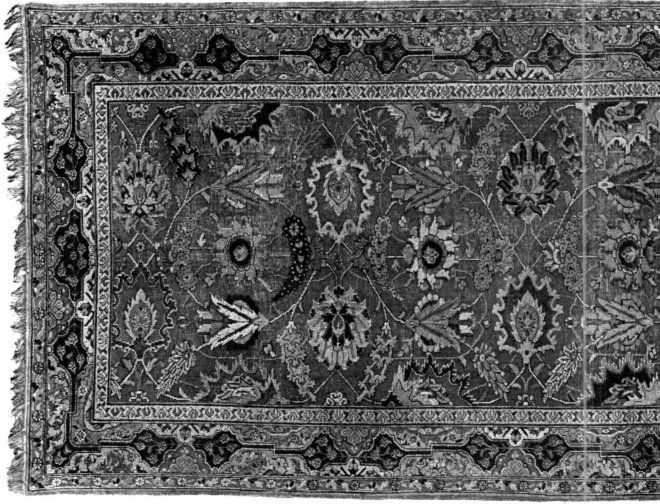

ABOVE: Border of the carpet on the preceding page. BELOW: India.
About 1600.

Arabesque carpet from Persia. 16th century.

Asia Minor. End of the 18th century.

Persia. 16th–17th century.

North Persia. About 1550.

North Persia. First half of the 16th century.

North Persia. Mid-16th century.

"Armenian" carpet from the Caucasus. End of the 17th century.